Nick Twemlow

About the Author

ANDREW FELD holds an M.F.A. in poetry from the
University of Houston and has received a Wallace
Stegner Fellowship from Stanford University. His
other honors include a James Michener Foundation
grant and a "Discovery"/*The Nation* award. A widely
published poet, his work has appeared in *Agni, The
Nation, New England Review, The Paris Review, Poetry,
Triquarterly, The Virginia Quarterly Review, The Yale
Review,* and many other journals. He lives in Eugene,
Oregon.

The National Poetry Series was established in 1978 to ensure the publication of five poetry books annually through participating publishers. Publication is funded by the late James A. Michener, the Copernicus Society of America, Edward J. Piszek, the Lannan Foundation, the National Endowment for the Arts, and the Tiny Tiger Foundation.

2003 Open Competition Winners

Stephen Cramer of Astoria, New York, *Shiva's Drum*
Chosen by Grace Schulman, published by University of Illinois Press

Andrew Feld of Eugene, Oregon, *Citizen*
Chosen by Ellen Bryant Voigt, published by HarperCollins Publishers

Raymond McDaniel of Ann Arbor, Michigan, *Entrance to Murder and After*
Chosen by Anselm Hollo, published by Coffee House Press

John Spaulding of Phoenix, Arizona, *The White Train*
Chosen by Henry Taylor, published by Louisiana State University Press

Mark Yakich of Oakland, California, *Unrelated Individuals Forming a Group Waiting to Cross*
Chosen by James Galvin, published by Penguin Books

CITIZEN

POEMS

Andrew Feld

Perennial
An Imprint of HarperCollins*Publishers*

HarperCollins books may be purchased for educational, business, or sales promotional use. For information please write: Special Markets Department, HarperCollins Publishers Inc., 10 East 53rd Street, New York, NY 10022.

FIRST EDITION

Designed by Nancy Singer Olaguera

Library of Congress Cataloging-in-Publication Data

Feld, Andrew.
  Citizen: poems / Andrew Feld.—1st ed.
    p. cm.
  ISBN 0-06-072603-2 (pbk.)
    I. Title.

PS3606.E385C57 2004
811'.6—dc22   2004046451

04 05 06 07 08 ❖/RRD 10 9 8 7 6 5 4 3 2 1

for Pimone

Acknowledgments

Grateful acknowledgment is made to the editors of the following publications in which some of the poems in this book first appeared, sometimes in slightly different versions:

Agni: "Great Hill Lyric"; *American Literary Review*: "Two Chapters," "Opium Poppies I," "Opium Poppies II," "Zealot"; *The American Scholar*: "Paper Weight"; *The Canary*: "C.," "Intermission"; *The Formalist*: "Personal"; *Gulf Coast*: "Late-Breather"; *Michigan Quarterly Review*: "Best and Only"; *The Nation*: "Used by the Kind Permission of . . ."; *New England Review*: "Abstract for a Burning City," "Signature," "Song," "To Adam"; *The Paris Review*: "Not Included in This Landscape," "Talking with My Father About God"; *PN Review*: "Ice Age"; *Poetry*: "The Drunk Singer I"; *Triquarterly*: "Dedication"; *The Virginia Quarterly Review*: "The Drunk Singer II," "On Fire"; *Western Humanities Review*: "They Have a Name for It"; and *The Yale Review*: "The Boxers," "Crying Uncle."

"Dedication" also appeared in *The 2004 Pushcart Prize XXVIII*, edited by Bill Henderson (Pushcart Press, 2004).

"Song" also appeared online in *Born* (www.bornmagazine.org) as a collaboration with the artist A. J. Dimarucot.

With love and thanks to my parents and family for their support and belief, and my deepest gratitude to my teachers and the insightful readers of this manuscript: Rick Barot, David Ferry, Linda Gregerson, Corey Marks, Robyn Schiff, and Nick Twemlow. Special thanks to the James Michener Foundation, the Wallace Stegner Program at Stanford University, and the Yaddo Corporation for their generosity. And beyond all expression, my gratitude for selecting my book to the National Poetry Series and Ellen Bryant Voigt.

Contents

The National Poetry Series was established in 1978 to ensure the publication of five poetry books annually through participating publishers. Publication is funded by the late James A. Michener, the Copernicus Society of America, Edward J. Piszek, the Lannan Foundation, the National Endowment for the Arts, and the Tiny Tiger Foundation.

2003 Open Competition Winners

Stephen Cramer of Astoria, New York, *Shiva's Drum*
Chosen by Grace Schulman, published by University of Illinois Press

Andrew Feld of Eugene, Oregon, *Citizen*
Chosen by Ellen Bryant Voigt, published by HarperCollins Publishers

Raymond McDaniel of Ann Arbor, Michigan, *Entrance to Murder and After*
Chosen by Anselm Hollo, published by Coffee House Press

John Spaulding of Phoenix, Arizona, *The White Train*
Chosen by Henry Taylor, published by Louisiana State University Press

Mark Yakich of Oakland, California, *Unrelated Individuals Forming a Group Waiting to Cross*
Chosen by James Galvin, published by Penguin Books

III

IV

I

On Fire

Having been taught by fools, how else could I have ended up
but as I am? a man who panics at the sound of his own voice,
a blusterer, afraid that within the five-pointed maple leaf there lies
another name he never knew; ready, always, to be found wrong.

Listen: in my tenth year they put me in a room where one plane
watched another plane fly over a city. It was morning in both
places. In black & white at first the explosion looked like water
rising. Captured, they say, on film, as in: pulled out of time

so we can rewind it and watch it happen again, as in a memory,
as in: this is a memory we all have, these are our family pictures.
There was that kind of shame. As if the fire really had been stolen.
And sitting on the floor there was one boy who even earlier

that year came home to find his mother hanging from a rope
in the kitchen. What didn't he know that he needed this film
to teach him? Already what he knew was enough to terrify
the teachers, so that they couldn't look at him. But they also

couldn't not look at him. As if he was an obscene pleasure.
And he was beautiful. Complete. But what he carried in him
seeped out as hate for anyone of the same sex as his mother.
It was that simple: even a fourth-grade mind could understand.

So the girls stayed away. And from the other side of the common room, where the books full of numbers being added, subtracted, and divided were kept, our new teacher watched, helpless, knowing he also needed this knowledge, but she couldn't give it to him.

Which might be why she let me touch her. Because she couldn't get near him and my head against the antique white lace of her dress was a good enough *almost*. Her hair was light brown, if I remember correctly. *Innocent* is supposed to mean *free from hurt*

but it can also mean you don't know what you're doing. As when I felt that touching her wasn't enough and I wanted to press closer, until someone felt pain, or until I passed through her dress and found

myself inside her. It didn't matter if she was an adult and I was ten:

what I wanted wasn't sex. Or not what I have learned to think *sex* is. Her dress was made of a material called *vintage,* which meant that although it had managed to avoid all the minor catastrophes of red wine stain and hook snag, along with the major disasters

of history, no one had treated the cloth with chemicals, to make it flame retardant. And on the whole length of the hand-sewn inner seam
that started at her wrist and ran all the way down to her ankle, no one had remembered to place even one small label warning:

if you touch the sleeve of this garment to the still-hot coils of an electric stove, it will explode. Which is what happened. There's the kind of scream you hear in movies. What I heard twenty-seven years ago didn't sound anything like that. It was

sharper and can't be recorded. No matter how many times
you rewind the film. You keep going back and each time
there's a little less there. Until the memory has become
the event. And how you feel about the memory. The materials

have burnt away. There was so much fabric and all of it on fire.
Her hair too, which was long, as I remember. She came running
from the faculty kitchen, as if she could escape what she was
turning into. But all she did was excite and encourage the flames.

Ice Age

The sharp face of Mt. Olympus rises
above the glacial cape wrapped around
its neck: a climber's paradise, which I'm not
skilled enough to ascend. So I hike on
a ridge on the other side of the valley,
at a lesser though still great height, balanced
between the green and white—the rain forest
below me on my left, and on my right
a glacier, blinding in the August sun.
I stop to drink and, because I'm living
a clumsy life, drop my water-bottle cap
into the *bergshrund*—the gap where the ice
has pulled away from the mountain wall.
What happens next? Do I go in thirst among
the rocks, or walk carefully holding my water
upright? No. Instead, I lower myself
down into the real abyss. This happened.
I down-climbed through the day. The light turned blue,
then milky white, then a dark gray. The rock
in my hands was slick from the melting glacier.
I slipped, and fell, and clung, then slipped again
and stuck. Thirty or forty feet below the surface,
the snow was black with dirt and hard. Years,
millenniums, of weather were piled above me.
Who comes back from these places? Alive, down
there I thought *old world, new world,* and *so,
this is where the time goes.* But, mostly:

what, exactly, is the stupidest thing
I've ever done? Just what was beneath me?
A frozen field, with small, unnamed flowers,
caught in the summer when the snow fell
and didn't melt. Ever. As though at the ocean
a wave came in and stayed. And then another.
And so. The water walking up its own steps.
Is it better to freeze or drown? I up-climbed;
but even in the heat and green life of the rain
forest, where mosses hang on all the trees,
I still felt cold. In my mind, snow was falling
and sticking. It starts. Again. It's starting now.

The Drunk Singer I

sits on the curb outside the bar and sings,
her legs stretched out into the town's one street.
She wasn't even halfway through her second set,
deep in her cloud of first- and second-hand smoke,
when all the interruptions become too much:
the man who shook the telephone and yelled
he still deserved *at least* another chance,
and closer, the constant advances of the idiot questioner,
who wanted to know where she'd been all his life—
all these rough drafts, desperate for revision,
forced her to take her insulted act outside,
into the first cold winds of late October,
which slam summer shut and lock the storm windows
in place, in all the houses over the bay.

Taking her place among the idolaters
of might-have-been, she picks the song back up
and starts her effort at correction; or else
she's just indulging in the private pleasure
of owning such a strong mouthful of voice.
From where she sits, her head below our belts,
the harsh, thick-throated gutturals come up,
are softened into slowly spoken labials
and rise to breathy aspirations. She's gone
far beyond the limits of her cover song,

—*I will always love you*—or some other lie,
into a quiet place where something broken
in bright scales is being disassembled
and then put back together, word by word.

Two Chapters

I. The Codex Huygens

Across the Grand Canal, water a vivid petro-green
the vaporetto takes us over, San Giorgio Maggiore
offers a façade "ideally suited to its island eminence"
—"giant stone, brilliant order, deep relief"—

and inside what is not white stone is painted white,

opening and illumining every corner of the "anachronistically
classical" mid-cinquecento interior. And farther down
the central hall, a man is talking to his wife, slowly,
patiently, as one would to a fool, or a room full of students

 (in another ceremony they say: *To the young who ask,*

we explain. To the slow, we explain slowly). What can
she think, being talked to that way, for what, a lifetime?
Like a bird beating against the sharp-pitched rafters of an attic,
his voice fills the empty white above his head, the vaulted nave,
bereft of decoration. *There is one law only*: the shapes things take

is a reflection of that law. Not wrong, but wrongheaded,
to think that we, eavesdropping so late in the history
of their life together, can or could know anything about them.
It has nothing to do with us. *Transept,* he says, *altar, nave*.

Diapason, diapente, diatessaron: music, translated into space:

because the harmony of the world is expressed in seven numbers,
and the ratios between these numbers contain not only
all the musical consonances but also the inaudible
music of the heavens and the structure of the human soul.

There is only one law: Pythagorean, Biblical, Platonic.

The shapes things take is a refection of this law, which Palladio
used to build a kind of vaulted, mathematical perfection, in which
a man's voice echoes, talking to his wife, who is, as it turns out,
sick and weak and hangs on him. He is talking slowly because

she is too tired to listen and he wants to distract or entertain her.
It has nothing to do with us, the slow, deliberate voice,
explaining the law that built the perfect space it beats against,
the empty white it hits and echoes back against, to him.

Awful, and unasked for, these sudden, sidelong glimpses of the self.

II. *Fresno Street*

Here, the bad August heat is portioned out
unevenly. Which is to say, *unfairly*. On one,
the even side of the block, there are the elms,
those green constructions of the civic mind,

planted in just proportion so many feet apart,
the branches and the canopy under whose arbor
we find such shade. And here, on the other, odd
side of the street, these poor parodies, saplings,

spindly sticks propped by planks and wire.
Again, we're called to see error, in one
of its many forms. We call it loss, although
here are other words for what happened here

(incompetence, wrongdoing.) The crew the city
brought in to cut away the first appearance
of the Dutch disease were in a rush. They wanted
to get the job done a little quicker and get home,

but they did not, as the regulations required,
sterilize their tools, their shears and saw blades,
after each operation, as you would in any
operation; and so the disease, *Ceratocystis ulmi,*

which had been seen on only one tree, a blotch
of fungus and a few dark beetles, was spread
by their ministrations, down the odd-numbered
side of the street, for the three blocks under

their care. *They didn't know the law*. Or, being
young and in a hurry, badly trained & underpaid,
thought they could bend it just enough
to slip under, and, for once, evade its exactions.

The city had to hire another crew, of older hands,
who worked in their good time, bringing to earth,
branch by lowered branch, a summer's worth
of shade. They hauled away the trunks & limbs

of pale, smooth bark and all the serrate leaves,
just then entering into their full season dark,
and left us with the same shame, equally divided
among everyone who lives here: an awkward

new brightness that leaves us blinking
at each other in the street. The trees
are gone, and in the place of where they stood,
a brilliant vacancy, fading into the light we know.

The Boxers

Here, in the middle of all this Houston heat, the two
sixteen-year-old featherweights step-by-stepping around
a center which should be large enough to hold them both

are working out, with painful, close attention, a number
of terrible ideas. The heat in here is an idea: it has a purpose
and a taste: it tastes like mile after mile of train passing

by the chicken-wired windows, the endless linked cars
full of what you don't know. The idea is that suffering
teaches you to suffer well, as though the end result

of dehydration isn't the skin & kidneys closing up
until what the body holds turns toxic, but the appearance
of something new willed into the blood, made of pain,

which you can then direct at the only person in the building
as beautiful as you are. Although of course there's nothing
sexual about this, the brief embrace of two boys, wet

with the same water you'd find at the bottom of any ocean.
And from the benches their plain-faced girlfriends watch, deep
in their impenetrable adolescence. As if all this were on TV,

as normal as the newsman saying *a train carrying industrial
waste has derailed and is burning outside the city,* and the simple
precautions: *Stay indoors. Close your windows. Don't breathe.*

But these two boys are in it, the sweat washing down
their stomachs and backs rinsing the black air off their skin,
turning the absurd abstractions of last night's news

into visible concentric rings around the waistbands
of their nylon Everlast shorts, as if all this was designed
to be a further test of their endurance, or show us

how even while you sleep your body can be making
serious mistakes, taking in lungful after lungful
of other people's errors. The soaked fabric sticks

to their thighs so closely you can see the hairs
underneath and the moving weave of muscle and almost
the tight string stitched through the overlapping plates

of stomach muscle and cinched tight between them,
drawing them closer until the old men outside the ring
begin to shout they didn't come here to see lovers

and another man comes in to pull them apart.

Description of Seas, Waters, Rivers, &c.

I walkt along a stream for pureness rare,
water spilling on stones, its passive voice
slipping, under, in. *Come, my robe will open*
fold after fold, surface after surface
more naked than any skin, alluring as
the idea of clear, cold thought sliding through
soft velvet life and smooth-slick rocks—but what
then hung the great root-bulbs and massive trunks
of Douglas fir on the banks like a train wreck?
What endless thirst pours down its own throat?
O dense translucence, smooth gears of the machine
spinning by the broken mattress of moss,
uncoiled springs of fern poking through, and trillium,
As kind companions in one union grows.
As autumn flesh contending with the sun,
the father puts his unread volume down, thumb
in place, and yells a warning to the child
rushing towards the grinding gears of surf.
What is the unread book they figure in
as marginalia, scrawled on the long white strip
of beach, that book where the blue page of ocean
meets the blue page of sky at the horizon,
and that dark wisp of cloud in the far corner,
which looks like a greasy thumbprint, and is—

Opium Poppies I

When my colors fell they cut my throat and dream
oozed from the cut, the full night's milk, the tar.

Even after a spit-slickened blade scraped clean
the incision and stole my sleep's ease, my un-

conscious in another body still hungered towards
the terraced slope it was sown broadcast in

as seed, where I grew as tendril pulled in two
directions, a string tying earth & air together.

Processed in another province and refined
into elements unrecognizable to myself,

no matter how many borders & states
I pass through, always invisible & illegal,

the dream always remembers the body, leaf
& stem, capsule & stigmatic surface, the release

of red silks spread in the companionable field,
the coming sleep it was supposed to fill.

Abstract for a Burning City

The dust of Babylon is in the air.

I

The hill rose hard and white, as we proposed,
and long vowels sighed in the marsh below,
a restless shadow-shape of *Ahs* and *Ohs*
combing the grasses back; and on the exposed
surface, the wind drew scales on bronze water.

II

A speechless voice cried out to us; as if a hurt,
like Kafka's shame, could outlive its owner,
and circulate as spirit, an essence in the atmosphere,
a breath escaping through the harbor's mouth,
although that mouth was long since filled with dirt.

III

Somewhere below the oldest, the aboriginal sin,
an image with no shadow, lay waiting. Our tents
were pitched on the excrement of three civilizations;
the woman who said *my burning tears* and meant it;
the place where all broken promises end.

IV

At dawn, the single bearable day-lit hour, we left
our sleeping bags and from the cistern cranked up
buckets of the ancient stone-flavored water,
piercing the rose-petal surface with our cups
to pour knotted streams into the purifier.

V

Counting backwards from the trash of now,
we called the summit, the highest ground, *Zero,*
and scratched all day at ground baked hard as brick,
on our knees with a toothbrush and dental pick.
Everything was hopelessly involved with dust.

VI

We finally found what we were looking for
thirteen feet down: half-calcinated bones,
a bed of cinders running like a scar,
heat-twisted metal, broken glass, and scorched stones;
burnt by fires in the books that brought us here.

VII

Unearthed, their memorials were crudely carved,
but cleaned, the stones held the soft, fuzzed white
of motel corridors at four a.m., a carpeted fluorescence
leading to damp highways smeared with traffic lights,
where two cars wait to go in opposite directions.

VIII

That crow, dancing from newly excavated stone
to stone, a cautious catalogue of long-dead fires,
riddled our field days, always asking *after*:
what comes after *after*? with tilted cinder eye
askance at our slow work. *Once burnt, twice shy.*

IX

We found the jeweled robe of the bird-priest,
breastplate and heavy sleeves reddened with rust
and bronze bird-head. The outfit frightened us:
the hard stone eyes, sullen with atavistic will
and sharp, serrated feathers, flared for the kill.

X

Fearing nature, they banned the third dimension;
inventors of the alphabet, in our mouths they left
scraps of psalm and the ashy taste of lamentation;
sown in salt, preserved, a memory descends stone steps
to these houses, and lives; in spite of our occupation.

Dedication

We argued about the difficulty of degree,
the exhibitionist on stage, flaunting
his fluent ease, his keyboard mastery.
Poor puppet, beating at his box of strings.

We wanted more, didn't we?—a deeper adeptness,
the border between performance and performer
blurred, erased. It was for this we put our best
demeanors on and took our student seats
under the three jutting concrete tiers, beneath
the full-priced tickets. We sat in a concentrate
of time, as in the way the house lights dimmed,
the great candelabra reduced to three bronze dots
ellipsing on the Steinway's burnished wood,
a trill announcing the Divertissement,
Etude, Nocturne, the concert hall reduced
to a small room where a young man sits
trying a few notes out, each tentative thought
hanging in his head like a pocketful of change
scattered on a white plate, the bright possible
in a dark room, gleaming, unchosen, tentative,
while in the bar below a woman waits
for him, the only woman in the bar.
She lets the men there buy her drinks, a glass
of vin ordinaire, maybe a Johnnie Walker Red,
and flirts, knowing what all these workmen think
of her, and her boyfriend. They think he has
the easy life, and that she is the easy life.

She likes their envy and their scorn; it fits
her like a soft, clinging woolen skirt
and makes her feel as if her life was composed
by choice, not accident. The piano player
renders all this a little too stiffly,
with too much distance, insufficiently
rubato, the notes hanging in tight clusters,
a sheaf still waiting for the whetted scythe
as two headlights sweep across another mile
of Illinois wheatfield. The vehicle
is now the smaller room of a compact
heading home, content in the ordinary.
So when the wished-for place arrived, as if
a car radio suddenly started to play
the memory of a music heard in a dream,
it was our brilliance, alone, to recognize
the moment that fulfills a lifetime's work,
the long sequacious notes stretching like lines
across a field of shifting, bowed heads,
bringing the unthought-of, unknown to us,
music and musician dissolving in union,
and then, consummated, the harvest in,
milled down and shipped away; and in a room
with the lamp dimmed, the lid of the keyboard
clamped shut, the couple lie in bed together,
eating torn-off pieces from the loaf of good bread
two coins taken from the white plate bought them,
while the music starts moving through a succession
of rooms, each one larger and more expensive,
until the piece is finished. Then the musician
stops, waits, and bows: once to the applauding crowd
and once to the now-silent instrument.

II

Late-Breather

But words came halting forth . . .
He came from there not red and howling his one note
like all the rest. And so we had to worry. For years
he didn't cry. Or speak. Until, with such strange fears
and panic-quickened hearts, our senses finally woke
to what he meant. So long unheard he'd spoken in
the thirty-seven different dialects of rain
and all the languages of frost, shrinking in sun
or growing scratch by scratch upon the windowpane.

We'll wait. And when he finds the fragile hiss of mist
no longer answers to his growing needs, we'll tell
him what to say, instead of the thing itself. We'll twist
his tongue around our consonants and syllables.
We'll force our language down his throat, until he spits
it back at us. He'll have to take our words for it.

Crying Uncle

The sun is empty. Behind that great husk of light,
those brilliant surface-effects, a brutal, cold wind
of memory—Siberian, Tartar, *Poilische*—cuts through
the thin sweaters old Jewish men wear in Arizona,

cashmere, in bright shades of sherbet: orange, raspberry,
lemon, and lime. And thinner, softer than the sunset-cloud-
colored fleeces which adorn them, are their names,
which are retired now and wait, impatiently, for nothing.

My father's name is Maury. He had three brothers:
Meyer, Bernie, and Marvin, all now deceased. As dead
weights on the page my desk lamp cranes its neck
to light upon, they file into the dark of an empty theater,

where the handwringing and grandiloquent gestures,
the gaslights and greasepaint, *Shylock's Daughter*
and powdered hair, where even the language has become
an embarrassment. And I'm working late with nothing

but these names to go by. Because I'm sitting shivah here,
and my lamp is a soul, *animula,* little wanderer, and this is
the House of Mourning. For Meyer in Los Angeles,
a traffic engineer who changed his name to Myron X. and left

his television on day and night, for Marvin in Phoenix,
a landscape architect, and for Bernie, the man who set
the Doomsday Clock, a physicist: Manhattan Project,
Los Alamos, then MIT and *The Bulletin of Atomic Scientists*.

Their bodies and ashes are strewn across the continent:
Los Angeles, Phoenix, New York. In death they have been
utterly assimilated. And if they reentered this world,
stripped clean of their Poland of Memories, of Isaac Babel's

"dense melancholy of Sabbath eves," their old men's bodies,
soft, sloping shoulders, their cancers and bad hearts,
what then? Would they come back holding little mirrors
and puff-pads, almost-angels in white laboratory coats,

scented of *Eternity* and offering, for next to nothing really,
to erase the years from around your eyes, flashing
your own face at you as if it was a postcard from hell,
or would their transmigration take a wayward course,

treading again the ancestral paths of exile, through suburbs
of K- and Wal-Marts, limbo-landscapes the imagination
cannot stick to, until angry and complaining
they emerge from the long tunnel of birth. Am I them?

Meyer, Bernie, Marvin: one, two, three steps of a man
coming up from underground, sliding each shoe
over the worn steel lips of the subway stairs and holding
tightly to the handrail until, reassured by sound and feel,

once again he's walking the streets of his childhood.
They haven't cleaned the store windows but inside
leather and paper have turned to plastic and the language
that replaced his has been replaced by yet another.

No one remembers him now except the Cossack
lying on his newspaper bier, the one on the vodka bottle,
and the scholar of mislaid origins, bent all night over
a book with letters printed the same color as the paper,

words his pen uncovers one by one. It's slow going,
even with the cone of light pouring on the page
as a refrain, a trope of memory borrowed from
the extravagant fires we started with, and the figure

paused outside the window, waiting to hear his name
lifted back into life, through the sour medium
of my late-night breath. The wind in last year's leaves
sounds like static. The silence between us is complete.

Two Family Sonnets

I. Talking with My Father About God

Above us, on the second floor, my mother's
footsteps creaking fall. When we die, that's it.
He looks heavenwards: what's up with dinner?
What? No, no, there is no god. The subject—
or maybe it's just me—distresses him.
He'd rather talk about what I plan to do
with my life. Time is short, and passing, in
this world that's all we've got. I'm thirty-two

and I am not, God knows—I hope—trying
to pass on to him, bearded, distant, the blame
for the shape my life has taken, or denying
responsibility. God is the name
we give to all the things that scare us most:
how we live, and what happens when we don't.

II. Personal

SJM, at 35, looks unimportant
and just might be, seeks—what?—not an *other*
but some kind of transformation. The mirror
shows me only a perpetual student,
the forehead rising like a wall I can't
break through. The narrow face comes from my mother
and shows the Parry side, spendthrift scholars
who had a habit of dying young. I didn't.
And in the eyes, water, and something evasive:
my father's frugal worries, fears, and regrets,
come to regard the reckless way I live,
which all my books can't help me change, with debts
rising beyond anything I'll ever earn,
while learning what I never asked to learn.

The Drunk Singer II

Later now, in the year and in her voice,
with her band all occupied in boxing up
their dismal instruments, the sorry woods
and worn-out brasses that kept them so absorbed
three sets into the night, so she works on
her rum and Diet Coke and pages through
the windswept Fake Book of her mind, as if
she still could fit the moment to its song
with such a pitchy voice, the strain of trying
to fill an empty house at closing time
bending each note a little off the mark,
while she wonders if she's *Crazy, for being
so blue,* and just *How Blue Can You Get,* before
deciding either *Too Blue* or *Almost Blue.*

And on the fogged-in highway home, the man
who's had too much is listening to the noise
of noise, the wheels-on-wet-sand sound of stations
missed, and finding that his teeth aren't sharp enough
to scrape off his tongue the taste of corn and wheat
wrung through the digestion of a Tennessee
distillery, as he moves deeper into the in-between,
this patch of low-lying November weather, and worries
at his radio, pushing all the little silver knobs
again and again and again, each effort corrected

immediately by the next, the same mistake,
the same grains of static released at every point,
until he shuts the whole thing off and hears
nothing, in its diminished form, continuing.

Intermission

As always, the music was divided   into two unequal
halves: first three new pieces   making their dissonant
debuts, and then the Brahms   symphony the evening
was advertised as. In the fifteen   minutes between,
as jarring notes resolved into   familiar tones of talk,
I watched a woman walk   across the lobby, spot-lit
by her local celebrity. To be   blunt: I stared at her
breasts, two loaves of blue-white   skin pushed up by
a green gown, with a stone   in the cleft. I followed
the angle of everyone's attention   and there she was,
the bad press of her breakup   unrolling a few steps
of carpet in front of her. It was   a good story, if you
weren't her. There were estates   on three continents
and an island, injuries measured in   the long numbers
banks use, and an element someone   wanted to own
all of. Fire, or air. Of course   I'm exaggerating. All
they wanted was the silver   she kept liquid inside her
veins. I mean her story was   personal, like history,
and public, like good gossip.   A ship set free from its
scaffolding she glided through   the room, carrying a
small blue pool over the emerald   carpet, liquid and
spilling its light the infant's   fist-sized brilliant she
carried away between   her breasts when she put her
old name on the papers   and the decision was final.
To make a diamond like this,   she told the press on
the courthouse steps, *you   take two hundred and fifty
pounds of dirty money   and squeeze it between your*

legs. But the diamond was so clean light blinked passing through and her return to the name she had grown up in was like a baptism in its waters. Or so I hope. It's easy to hate the indecently rich. And the name she renounced means *blood-sport,* which means a stag trying to outrun an arrow in its neck. Of course I might have been misinformed about who she was and the stone spilling its eaux-de-vie inside the square neckline of her green gown, glass, not a brilliant example of the damages she was entitled to. But the line of fire flicking from facet to facet inside the pear-shaped pendant seemed real, a gem-cutter's art turning our common glances into an ecstatic light counterpointing itself, our looking made visible as sparks on her skin. The suits and dresses crowded around the bar stared star-struck at the stone in her cleavage as she walked by, lifting their glasses up as the current which carried her towards the now-open double doors rose over their waists and the recessed ceiling lights blinked in three sets of three, to signal that the music would continue with, or without us.

They Have a Name for It

Of course. So when the season was called off
and all the summer people packed up their money
and headed north, south, west, and to the east
the Atlantic drags itself back and forth across
the same small stretch of beach, I stayed in the bar
named after a politician and joined the chorus
of malcontents. *Moon-cussers,* my friend told me,
after their ancestors, who, on nights exactly like this,
when it could rain or snow, when anything,
it seems, could come in on the wind,
assembled by driftwood bonfires and drank hard
liquors, rums, probably, made by slaves
in the British West Indies, while waiting
for the merchants' ships to join them.

At this point I would like to state my solidarity
with the working classes. Which isn't easy.
Because every morning there would be the same
seals' bodies washed up on the shore. *Washashore*:
the words the locals use for anyone whose parents'
parents weren't born here. And in the water,
hiding behind the waves, the dark, wet hair,
the slicked-back dancers' heads of the living
animals. Because what the locals haul up
in their nets they kill, with competition sharpening
so many knives, and dwindling stocks. Still,
the crime *is* against nature, and so great

that just to move their bodies on the sand
costs more than you could ever afford.

When all my friends shut their doors against
the cold, going out only to get videos or drunk,
and the sun, with all its wealth of heat, moved
to the farthest point away, I sold my days
for eight dollars an hour and was glad to get it,
filling the back reaches of the Pamet Marsh
with the small engine of my unskilled labor,
clearing away the litter of fallen locust trees.
At the first breath of winter their shallow roots
fail and they fall face-forward, sighing. And in
the Governor Bradford, the man washed down
his last complaint and put his empty shot glass
on the bar. If you have to know, he said, don't
ask me. He said I don't know I just live here.

Three Things

I. Paper Weight

Brought home from the museum gift-
shop in the long darkness that ended
when I opened my eyes to this world,
mock scarab of metal nicked and pitted
to make it look like what we think
it should resemble, the smooth, flat base
and brown-black bronzed patina hold
a finer cold than the hard stone original
ever could have, waiting out history
in the chest of its owner, to remind
the dead heart not to betray the body.
Talisman or temple token of the dung
beetle, *scarabaeus sacer,* whose image,
as verb, was sacred, signifying both
become and *create,* the replica now
sitting on my father's desk, a weight.

II. The Poems of Dylan Thomas
    New Directions, 1971

Alive as grass or mold, the lime-green cloth
of the hardcover breaks through the badly foxed
and frayed dust jacket. The pages too are stressed:
dog-eared, the tips bent back; and penciled in,

the childish scrawl of my bad handwriting
shadows his metaphors, trying to track
the bright coeval sun that followed him
from Prologue to unfinished Elegy.

III. Signature

Mine, this sprawl
of bent saw-teeth,
a crumpled line
left at the bottom
of the sheet, legal
and indecipherable.
Mine, this mess, less
a collection of letters
from any alphabet
than a dark string
dropped on the page.
Mine, this scrawl,
not the full-formed
cursive script which
the educated man
once made his mark
with, but a presence
on the paper, pure id,
insisting *mine, mine,
mine,* the unteachable
inner child clawing
his way back out,
affixing the page,
the check, the document,
with my hand, my print.

Not Included in This Landscape

are any houses. That's for sure. And as for
cars, trucks, tractors, trailers, motorcycles,
you're in another universe, friend. At most
we would allow a dirt road, seedy, unkempt,
to walk across the marsh and fizzle out,
diffused into a field. We could tolerate that.

It still might be possible to have a hill
although it's certainly a risk—and we're not big on risks,
anymore. But it would be worth it
to see the marsh and the marsh birds, hawks, heavy-winged,
rising with feet full of mice and crying triumph.
We could surround ourselves with hills.

Should there be an ocean? We could accept
a flat bay with a weak edge tapping the shoreline,
like impatient fingers on a tabletop.
We have seen all we need of storms:
the heavy wave lifted to slap the face of a friend,
the scene in the restaurant, the crying jag in the passenger seat.

And what else? Nothing else.
The airplane would fall into the sea,
beyond our horizon, and the lovers would stay at home:
they can perform their own indoor pastorals,
but it does not interest us. Here, our worries are more material:
the clattering of machinery, beyond the hills, demanding inclusion.

To Adam

All afternoon we said their names
as colors: red-winged, ruby-throated,
yellow-shafted, golden-crowned,
until, palate exhausted, we shifted
synesthetic into song and let them
be music, airy melismas falling off;
as one assured the unsaid, unstressed,
is understood (the note is *grace,*
the rhyme is feminine). So Eve
entered the picture as chiaroscuro,
a shadow-sheen on her bright shoulders
both complement and completion.
As one who pauses, passing
through room after room of quiet,
Giotto to Raphael to now, she waited
by the trembling waters, to see
the answer to that strange command:
in my image. What isn't? The steps
of those umbrella-pines, climbing
from sleep to the last, worn-thin light
of day, a faded sheet stretched
between two women who fold by fold
approach each other, as the work
of naming narrows to the finest brush,
a single mink bristle dotting a few
more details in. That intestinal thread
forced out of a toad's military belly,

an almost-acrylic of El Greco
or Soutine. A rented blue Hertz car
flees the scene, a *convertible,*
named after our most American hope:
what's that around the corner
we're about to become? Listen,
my first and oldest friend, even
with so much material, a continent,
between us, we might be working
in the same direction. We still
could turn out to be twins.

III

Great Hill Lyric

I

The walker there must soon eat his heart, Thoreau
said of this path, a thin line of white threading
through bayberry and poverty-grass, which led him
into what he called *futurity*: a dry, sun-stunned
landscape where plants barely rose above the shadows
their names cast, as he walked into the long view.

And then, as if to show that he was right in thinking
the essential mysteries must remain unsolved,
they broke the distance down, first into half
and three-quarter acre lots, and then the smaller
portions of five-by-seven picture windows
facing the more expensive waterfront properties.

Still, in little starts and stops, some fragments
of his path have kept their hold up on the hill
as *sites,* each opening like a word the tongue
stutters against until the sentence is forgotten,
small survivals the walker there now finds, skirting
the fact of these new subdivisions. Like the fox

I saw there once, shuttling her kits from one
person's property to another's. As sharp and quick
as a regret, she moved her limp mouthfuls
from the mown pasturage of Perry's Farm
to the as yet untenanted scrub farther up the slope,
slouching smoothly under the electric wires.

II

Strung between cracked white ceramic spools,
an aching hum hung through the late summer
afternoon, as power trembled into thought
and grew louder, until with the rifle-shot sound
of sound breaking, three jets in V formation
passed overhead. And just like that, the day

was separated into *before* and *after,* the pieces
falling the way the sky inside the church
must have fallen in Assisi, as Giotto's shivered blues
came down in the earthquake, falling
on both pairs, the two Franciscan friars
and the two fine-arts inspectors. What one pair

saw as beatific vision, the other knew
as painstaking restoration. But when it broke,
before it buried them, they might have had
a brief vision of the painted arms of saints
reaching out to them, while the imagined sky
of heaven cracked into a cloud of dirty white.

And then there was the outsized price tag
we always knew that visions come with:
twenty-eight miles of aluminum scaffolding
and half a dozen restorers sorting through
milk crates and plastic trays, trying to piece together
a single afternoon's bright clarity.

III

There was a time when I thought vision
could save me, or at least show me the person
I needed to become, in order to stop being
who I was. So with a friend I bought two hits
of a kind of drug they used to call
"consciousness-expanding," but which,

in the end, turned out to be only a bad thing
done to the brain. Stakes, spray-painted orange,
had already been driven into the hill, to mark
the places where the houses would be built.
And the promise *was* good: small
Windex-colored squares called windowpane,

each one like a good day's sky concentrated
down to the size of a computer chip.
But what we saw was—nothing: gaudy
and vibrant, as a twilight-yellow of stiff pages
unfolded down the slope in front of us,
in fields where loose strife, the import,

held up its purple bells and a few late birds
called to each other from inside the darkening
poplar stands. But still, nothing.
No messages from the world saying
Repent Before Using or instructions on how
to open the little white box I called my life.

IV

When the jets flew over the distant blue border
of the horizon and the noise of their engines,
traveling on a separate time-line, faded after them,
the fox unfroze from her terror and disappeared
into the landscape, the dead pine needle russets
and rust-colored sand in the gravel wash.

Then machines came and crawled all over the hill,
trailing black lines of burning tar and leaving houses
in the kind of sudden suburban sprawl
that happens between one year and the next.
Reduced to just a shade, the she-fox flits
on the edge of perception, a poor fugitive thought

hurrying through the end of summer. *It's time
to pack,* someone writes. They've already boarded up
the small train station and the couple on the bench
outside lean their thickly wrapped shapes together
as the beech forest settles into its long, archaic dream.
It's like that, only the story has been translated badly,

a stiff, ready-made phrase replacing the lucid chatter
wind makes in dry leaves, the original eloquence
of the landscape broken by the prefabricated shapes
of neat, new houses, or transcribed
into a minor key, as in the sound of sharp strands
of beach grass whisking against a walker's leg.

V

You think of Thoreau steering his solitudes
through the fields, common lands and small,
wind-stunted orchards of the Lower Cape, oriented
by compass, map, and his sense that the roads
men follow are only tracks which habit
and a slavish disposition keep us from straying from.

So it comes as a surprise to learn that he had
a companion, as I did, someone he might have
turned to, veering off the inner beach, to speak
nostalgically of home: the clean shirt waiting
on the bed, the bed with its coarse linens
folded back, waiting after a lazy bath and dinner.

Also lost are the companion's replies, his fretful
queries and exasperation as what he said
became just gull-cry and the bicker of smaller birds
over shreds of meat in a few broken shells
at the high-water mark. At best, his unwritten words
survive, like the numbers, initials, and love-data keyed

in Plexiglas, in the phone booth near the beach,
as useless commentary on a hermetic text.
The World as Our Beloved Codex: a book
the sun, that ancient scholar with one great thought,
tries to enlighten us on, stripping layer
after layer of dawn off of the broken gray asphalt

VI

where we stood, tired and burnt-out, speechless
as our morning opened into the clear light
of simple description. A man crouches on the lawn
of a cottage named after a flower and wrestles
with the awkward wing of a new sailboard,
his hard exhalations in time with a white curtain

breathing in and out over the sill, cloth hovering
like a feather over a dreaming mouth, until she wakes
and steps onto the porch, to shake the sleep
from her tangled brown hair the way wind trembles
in two scrub oaks next to her car, and the shrub,
bougainvillea, next to that, her arms and legs

radiant through her cotton gown, as in a vision
of the naked day, the woman unclothed by light.
All unfolding with the "beautiful clarity"
of a Russian poem from the last century,
where the metaphor—*and in the parking lot,
the day's heat already rose in slow Cyrillics—*

turns out to be not ornament or elaboration,
but the main theme's reappearance
in the final movement, when *a* can only equal *a,*
not as in the girl's mouth, scented like violet,
or the apple, which can be said to smell like love,
but blood, which only smells like blood.

Envoi

i

Poor landscape, rich with light & distance, when Thoreau
first saw it. Orleans to Eastham was a clear view
and the telegraph wires were a blessing for the birds.

ii

Suppose the first whistle, the *bob* of the bobwhite's call,
is not the chorus-preceding C but the note that brings
the whole house down, first crack in the farthest blue corner,

iii

walker with his staff of seasoned ash, setting off
into a maze which shatters before he finds the center.
Poor sojourner, with his ashen stick, peeled wand,

iv

a figure from a pack of cards found in an abandoned
amusement park. *The Woman Bearing a Glass of Water,*
windblown hair lashing at her cheek, the flimsy deck,

v

fox cutting across a field of dry brown grass, the couple
still waiting for their train beside the fractured carousel
and tilt-a-whirl, the whole dismantled carnival of summer.

vi

House of Broken Mirrors, in the new development,
streets named after memories no one has anymore,
labels on empty boxes a trespasser is sorting through,

vii

his asthmatic rasp behind boarded windows a sigh of fire
in the creek bed. Wayward misanthrope, iconoclast,
the path you took still steals across the hill, submerged

viii

beneath concrete and tar or rising now in shining steps,
dropped coins of broken light. Who walks here now
becomes a ghost. Even your footprints are not your own.

IV

Best and Only

I. The Ship of State

The way a carp's speckled brown and white head
flashes just below the surface of the Potomac
night waters, Richard Nixon's penis almost enters

the national consciousness, as a thin gold thread
of urine stitches him to an August night in 1973,
on the stern of the *Sequoia*. Standing beside him

is the Cuban financier Bebe Rebozo, who is also
pissing into the river. The image is a small shame
in the middle of many greater ones: the damp dots

on his pants as he shakes off with an awkward
drunk step back and zips up, the president pissing
on the Republic, over which he stands. Exposed

briefly before being pulled back below decks,
the two men are easy targets for anyone's
anger or condescension. Jowly and soft

with the executive spread of men in the era
before exercise was invented, their bodies
bulge oddly, pumpkin-like growths swelling

the crotches and stomachs of their pin-striped suits,
as if their own flesh had risen up against them.
For the marksman stationed near, their appearance

at his post is an allegation he'd die to deny. Eyes
trained to see elsewhere, he holds his cool
weapon and a bead drops from the little jungle

of his armpit as twin diesel engines steer the boat
past the riverbank where the hippie who jumps up
to grab a green Day-Glo Frisbee out of the air hears

their voices and mistakes the drunken laughter
of two old men in a boat for the drunken laughter
of two old men in a boat, unaware that History

is passing so close he's breathing its exhaust,
its strain of scorched fuels distinct for a few
seconds and then folded back into the ordinary

summer night smells of mass transportation
and river water. We now know on this particular
August night they're shifting funds, arranging payoffs

for the plumbers, and harassing Henry the Jew,
denying they've *even heard of* Cambodia, as they sail
several martinis outside anyone's jurisdiction.

For these and other crimes, may they be lodged
in the sulphurous cavern of Satan's anus forever.
But what of the genuine warmth all the biographers

agree burns between these two men, the actual,
human love they felt for each other: is it only
the gaseous fire of butane tentacles wrapping around

a bushel of asbestos logs in the below-deck bar's
mahogany dark, or is it the quicksilver spirits
in the funneled glasses they lift to each other,

a whisper of vermouth tasting like amnesia
in the gin's frostbitten false fire, the warmth
in each sip drawing them closer together?

II. From the Apocrypha of Bebe Rebozo

iii

Protesters under the cherry trees: notice
how each fallen petal rots from the inside
with a small brown dot on its delicate center-seam,
like a piece of used toilet paper:
so corruption is essential in us. It's in our guts.

vii

The young no longer dance.
Instead they *twitch,* as if
their electric guitars were electrodes
taped to their genitals. If only.

But their children will rediscover
the steps they abandon
and follow them back to us.

xii

Richard, I dreamed we walked the fine silver sands
shoring the Bay of Pigs, and there, beside your wing-
tip's tip, we found a gull poking its bill into the gills
of a still-living fish. Out in the surf, girls' voices called

for your attention, as Tricia and Julie came riding shoreward
on the crests of waves; and this length of scaled muscle
was eaten alive at our feet, drowning in our oxygen.

III.19— : An Elegy

Apollo. Bebe Rebozo. Beatniks.
The Car. Counting backwards.
Cold Warriors. The century
I was born in. Disney. The Great
Depression and Anti-Depressants.
Everest. The Evil Empire. Electric
light and atomic energy. Frost
at Kennedy's Inaugural. Fucking.
Free love. Gridlock. Harley-Davidson
and Hell's Angels. *Ho Ho Ho Chi Minh*.
The Ivory-billed woodpecker. The Iron
Curtain. Joke: how many right-wing
neo-conservative, conspiracy theory,
survivalist, NRA, MIA, VFW,
free-market, anti-establishment
radio-talk-show-host-loving loners
does it take to screw in a lightbulb?
The Killing Fields. Love Beads.
Love-Ins. Love Canal. The Mall
of America. Medical waste. Richard
Nixon. No one's home. The century
when Oral Sex came into its own.
The Overdose. *People*. Peaceniks.
Plutonium. Post-. Pop-. Plastic-wrapped
bundles of cocaine washing up
on Florida beaches. Queer theory.
Race. A small car like a stereo
on wheels, the Soul Singer's voice
tearing through paper speaker cones

the way the spirit is formed and deformed
by the flesh. The century of the Teenager.
Televangelists. Uncut. Unadulterated.
Vietnam. Watergate. World Wars. The X ray.
Yeah Yeah Yeah. Zen Koan. Ground Zero.

C.

Or if he always knew? Then
            in that light we'd read
his seeming-aimless drift   from state to state
as a favored guest at ease, during a time of festival or fête,
his host's estate a continent to wander room to room.

And it would be *decision*
            that placed him outside
the race of moneyed men,   as self-aware he'd watch
his luck play itself out at the gaming tables,
in hearts, in clubs, in diamonds, and in spades.

Then we, collusive to his line
            of thought, seduced, would feel
her finger running down his sleeve,   promising
a window will be left half-open for him
to climb into another night with the small voice

against his ear saying
            please, yes, again, and again
hear who he is   affirmed a wonder
in rising tones; although, yes, he is aware
that with each exploit he is becoming *a* or *the*

Casanova, as his name hardens
            into an identity,
something he wears   like the slip of silk
he tells her to keep on, a layer of remove
that slides between their skins, not a lie

but not quite the truth either.
                    Better. And when he wakes
in yet another aftermath   of rank gray sheets,
sprawl of sideways spilling breasts and all
last night's slick fluids turned to dried glue,

the careful music of her perfume,
                    sharp floral high notes
of violet and lily   blended with the lower musks
of ambergris and civet, descended now
to the animal pungencies of armpit and crotch,

he would welcome
                    each new revelation
of her closed-off self.   I insist on it.
Until, still warm with sleep, he finds himself
alone, outside the café, eating slowly,

for pleasure, not for appetite,
                    the first red hints of sun
lighting each tear-shaped cell   of a cut section
of orange held up on his tine-tips, the long carved spiral
of its peel shining on a plate of white bone china.

Opium Poppies II

Behind the scrambled pixels he talked to us
in two voices, one incomprehensible to us

aimed into the camera, pointing at his field,
the other aimed beyond, explaining the field

to the distant audience, explaining the flowers,
although since he never spoke of them as flowers

their pointless beauty had an edge. *Infection*
he said, and *disease,* as if the flowers were infected

& shared blood blooming in syringes, or, in the story
we saw last year, rows of red vials in cold storage,

bad blood given to French hemophiliacs by corrupt
health officials. *My government is corrupt*

and cruel, one said, in a CNN-neutral accent, *so I plant
the most profitable crop*. But the farmer *is* his plants,

or at least half of him is, up to his waist in flowers, red
filling half the screen like a glass half-filled with red

Kool-Aid, the rest of the screen butane or chlorine blue
backing him, a heightened chemical-sublime blue

his unknowable face is part of, borrowing its pitches
& pixels, as his voice climbs in speed, volume, and pitch

until we can't hear it, effaced entirely by the translator's
slow, affectless tone, like someone translating

peacock into hamburger. And then the man's face,
or the mixture of dirt, sky, & technology called a face

because its shifting, unstable elements ask
us to recognize it as us, behind the protective mask,

came close to the lens, making the screen a pool's
prismatic surface. On the other side of the pool

we crouched on our bed, bowing to the TV
as we ate, as if our postures were poor & vision

worse, or as if our patient years of watching
might finally be rewarded, as when we once watched

a sea otter's graceful play at the Newport Aquarium
turn awkwardly real, when it shattered the aquarium's

thick glass, swinging a rock held in both hands back-
wards over its head, as it swam on its back.

On the other side the guide touched the glass
like a Dutch boy or a mime, as through the clear glass

white cracks spread, making the wall more & more visible
& another element of its Olympic-sized cell visible

to the crowd of children, parents, & retirees there & to us
too, as the animal swung the rock towards us,

using its one technology to break the shell of its cage,
wet cat's-face impassive as the barriers of language

& species cracked with each metronomic contact
of rock on glass & the guide tried to make eye contact,

yelling the animal's human name—*Hunter! Stop!*
Bad Hunter!—until the otter, for its own reasons, stopped.

Leftovers

Start with my ex, Lori, lost in
the insane asylum where she works,
gray corridors mazing through
the nineteenth-century facility-on-a-hill
of brick and stone, prison house
stowed out of sight in the suburbs
where Lowell and Plath did time
when their minds went wrong. *Bad day*

she says when she gets home, *I had
to take him down, shit in his hair,
screaming.* Inmates I know of from their
stumblings off the steep-pitched ascent
to sanity. A shower and a cold glass
of yellow-gold Italian white
and she's fine, puts on her short black skirt,
her knock-me-down-and-fuck-me shoes.

Midnight and music makes us shout
the simplest phrases—*beer? bathroom!*—
her high heels out of place in The Rat,
where the bands we love play. *Dangerous
Birds, Throwing Muses, Scruffy the Cat.*
Three sets and encores with feedback
pitching higher until they kick us out,
the amplifiers' screech and roar carried

into the muted, distanced, cars and crowds
of Kenmore Square. An aftershock
of music I still hear as tinnitus, thin
thread of metal on metal winding between
my ears, struck surfaces of the world
ringing. At the other end of the register,
a stone hums to itself, an eye
opening in geologic time. But *no,*

Lori says, those voices are chemical,
the family clattering forks on plates,
air dense with triggers, until one word
catches, echoes into an episode.
The fighter-angel turns to you
his Rorschach-face and administers
the choke-hold, ink-blot wings rising
flood waters as the dam gives way.

And Lori, still lost in a corridor
identical to the one that led her here
(and on and on, as in mirrors),
opens a door in the maze-like
nineteenth century echoing interior
and steps, as through a parted seam
in the thin membrane of the mind
this building is, into nightmare.

Naked, her wineglass base balanced
high on her chest, she tries to fit
the scene into story and can't, her fabled
remove failing in the room full of
glass-stoppered jars on wooden shelves
from floor to ceiling, hundreds of jars
of tinctured brown formaldehyde, floating
sliced sections of cerebral cortex,

like giant chestnut wedges steeping
in coffee: brain samples from the insane
men and women who lived and died here.
And Lori's syntax stutters, the problem
woven into the words she has to use
to describe it, the way each jar's
yellowed label is signed, dead names
written in easy, elegant script.

The Breakup Party

The couple in the garage apartment dance
on broken glass, naked, impossible to count
the soft sticking kisses of their bodies'
contact, the flashbulb flicker and burst underfoot

a path they're following in the wrong direction
as far as they can go. We're back in Houston,
where the billion-watt bauble of skyline
means *money to burn* and the empty miles

of air-conditioned cool under the city whisper
waste and want not, as they sway
back and forth across the candle-lit kitchen,
dressed in their original outfits and past pain,

her cherubic feet sticking on green linoleum.
Maybe, says the man, *maybe,* says the woman.
The word neither one will open
their mouth wide enough to admit is *fault,*

a line of stress fracturing the room as a trail
of red wine dotted to exclamation
with a delicate shatter. So they open another
bottle and take two more glasses off the shelf.

It's two a.m., the hour when the driver says
I'm okay as he turns the key and the car explodes
into music, speakers breaking midverse
into a celebration of obsession slash compulsion.

And in the apartment, a bedside clock radio plays
a smaller, halfhearted version of the same song
and the couple waltz towards it, their bodies
conforming to the shape of what they carry

between them, as they continue their struggle
in another room, footprints of blood and wine
mingled following them as embers on
the sand-colored wood of the living room floor.

Used by the Kind Permission of . . .

for P.T.

Woken, at six a.m., by the dense mist of song
triggered by the sun's rising, we recognized
the first trick in that well-practiced sleight-of-hand
morning would unfold for us: those small dots
of clear light placed on the spider's web outside,
that shallow orange ribbon cut into the sandy drive.

And there were other signs, even when the afternoon
had been reduced to just the single mockingbird
and his sped-up, bad memory of other musics,
that acknowledgments remained unsaid, as when
you explained the discipline, the years of work
that gave such ease to the flippant conversations

in the movie we watched that night, the uncredited
studio-servitude which made possible that careful
choreography of speech—an art as lost now
as that which made the banks of glass flowers
in the Natural History Museum, the translucent
fibrous stalk of the iris, the fretwork of decay.

There, under fluorescent fixtures, a coelacanth,
deep in a silt of ancient brown formaldehyde,
turned its prehistoric eye towards the empty case
you said contained antique sunlight, or could be
a cenotaph for what can't be captured, as leaves
scratched at the window, pushed by restless air.

Zealot

The one who writes my history will be the one who wears a wire.
    It's always been that way. The phone rang all night but I
    did not answer. There are voices that when you hear them,
    must be obeyed. But I wasn't ready yet.

Bill-collectors, telephone-solicitors, friends, family, servants
    of the state, and other powers; I knew that the only one
    who matters was lying next to me asleep, my hand deep
    in the soft warmth of her breasts.

When I said there is one god only I meant my beloved is the
    blesséd
        name. In the vineyards of Ein Gedi we watched the F-14s
        perform their stomach-wrenching centrifugal displays,
        spiraling in formation. So much firepower, watching over us.

Later, we went shopping on the Via Dolorosa. Such bargains
    we found there! And us, with a whole lifetime's worth
    of savings, now ready to be spent. We ate fat-free sorbet
    and listened to World Beat: rai, reggae, soukous, hip-
    hop, klezmer, afropop, zydeco, and the latest indie-rock.

When I said *my beloved* I meant there is one god, only.
    Her skin is the color of wheat and her hips, gold
    hinges. I part the curtains of her labia with the tip
    of my tongue and say the tetragrammaton, her name.

What makes you think I haven't been anointed?

I returned from my time in the desert prematurely gray,
  the chalk-white dust of the empty cisterns in my
  hair and lungs. Because this is the one life,
  I will forgive nothing. In my aorta I still can feel
  the work hammers of the approaching enemy.

After the ritual bath and the three glasses of sweet dark wine
  the elders took me aside. *Another,* they said, *you must
  find another.* There is no other.

I will return to her in the cedar temple of the night
  and take her like Christ the groom returning
  to his bride the church. But this is not a parable.

Song

You'll sleep alone   for one full year   they say

because it takes   at least that long   to learn to hear

how each object   in your hands   sings in the pitch

of what it is   its singularity   the chipped white plate

you eat off every day   revealing   a shadow pattern

when shorn of all   alcoholic gloss   a darkening

web of cracks   woven through the glaze   the froth

on your toothbrush   waiting   while you notice

for the first time   the coarse pitted surface   under

the tap   a faint green scribble   outlining the shape

of where   the porcelain has worn away   and in

the mirror   your mouth   teeth blurred with Crest

but every pore   on your face   standing distinct

who is this?   as you learn   what it means to be

singular   and listen   because attention *is* a form

of prayer   to the sound   of the new season forming

as what was lost   begins again   the mind performing

its little resurrections   while the short days   begin

to open up   and fill with light   and the first song

the mother's voice   so long misplaced   or buried

in the evening air   is now untombed   and given

back to life   clothed in new sounds   new words

Notes

"Two Chapters." The italicized section in *The Codex Huygens* beginning "because the harmony of the world is expressed in seven numbers" is taken from Rudolf Wittkower's *Architectural Principles in the Age of Humanism.*

"Description of Seas, Waters, Rivers, &c." Title, first and fourteenth lines taken from the Christopher Marlowe poem.

"Abstract for a Burning City." Epigraph from Wallace Stevens, "The Little June Book."

"Late-Breather." Epigraph from Sir Philip Sidney.

"Great Hill Lyric." The Thoreau quote which starts the poem is from *Cape Cod.* "The world is our beloved codex" is from Sir Frank Kermode, *The Genesis of Secrecy.* The last three lines of section VI are a retranslation of poem 17 from Jane Kenyon's *Twenty Poems of Anna Akhmatova* ("Wild honey has the scent of freedom").

CPSIA information can be obtained at www.ICGtesting.com
Printed in the USA
LVOW040737051212

310005LV00002B/57/P